CUPID'S POISON
ARROW
CAROL G. WELLS

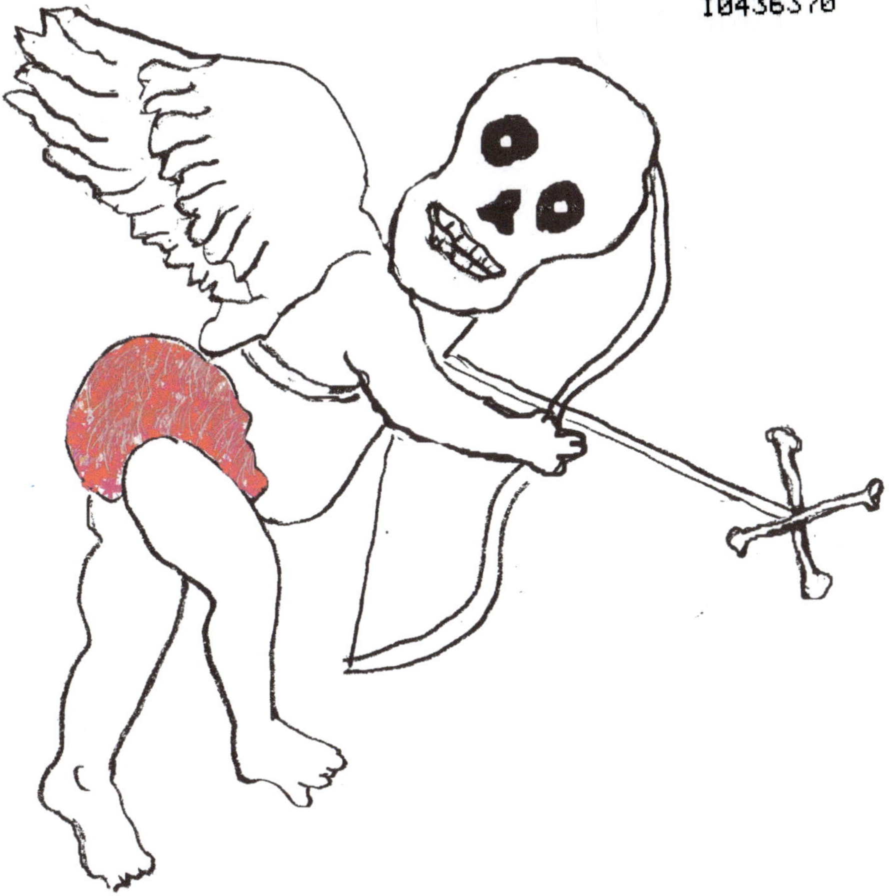

CUPID'S POISON ARROW:
Tips For Lovers

INTRODUCTION

There is an intoxicating, addicting drug cocktail lurking in your body right now. You can't get it on a street corner, you can't buy it over the counter or by prescription, and the FDA does not regulate it. It is, in fact, both free and legal. You don't snort it, inject it, smoke it, or huff it. Its biggest pushers are writers, musicians, poets, filmmakers and advertisers. It's high will make you giddy, optimistic, cockeyed, impulsive, irrational, and obsessive. Take it away and you feel sick with vomiting, shaking, uncontrollable crying, insomnia, and loss of appetite; it might even make you suicidal.

What is this potent, absolutely free drug? The *Love Cocktail*, a mixture of potentially intoxicating and toxic chemicals© that flood your body when you've been shot with Cupid's Arrow. The myth is that the arrow pierces your heart. The truth is that it impales itself in your brain.

The 17 pages that follow are designed to help you understand and cope with the overwhelming powers of the most sought

---

♥ Adrenaline, dopamine, serotonin and oxytocin are the main components.

after drug cocktail in the world. Keep reading and you'll discover:

- ✓ What happens in your brain when you fall in-love.
- ✓ Why you lose all sensibility.
- ✓ The role of lust.
- ✓ The difference between sexual arousal and sex drive.
- ✓ The difference between love and attachment.
- ✓ How it's possible to be in love with more than one person at a time.
- ✓ Why love does not conquer all.
- ✓ Why you are attracted to a particular person.
- ✓ How to keep from making bad relationship choices.
- ✓ What the *Dumpee Flu* is and what you can do to get over it.

*Carol G. Wells is a marriage counselor and sex therapist. She is the author of *Right Brain Sex*, *Naked Ghosts* and the former syndicated newspaper column, *Your Sex Life*. She has appeared on Donahue, Oprah, Nightline, and Good Morning, America. She currently resides in San Diego, CA.

WARNING!

STOP READING IF:
- ✓ You're irrevocably committed to the mystery of romance.
- ✓ You believe in Genesis or Creationism and thus reject science.
- ✓ You believe you can have only one true love in a lifetime.
- ✓ You cannot delay immediate gratification, even for long-term happiness.

KEEP READING IF:
- ✓ You're not looking for easy answers.
- ✓ You're ready to swim upstream against the current of socially accepted concepts about love.
- ✓ You're ready to accept being human, with all the imperfections that implies.
- ✓ You have the guts to choose happiness over guilt.

What Was I Thinking*

If you haven't done something stupid in the name of love, then I don't live in your world. If you haven't asked yourself *What Was I Thinking*© then surely you were brain

---

♥ Hereafter denoted by

dead. If you haven't done something regretful, shameful, or just plain awful in a relationship, then ask yourself if you're being honest. If you haven't become physically sick and an emotional wreck because of love, then surely you're the exception, or you're too young or... more likely, you're too much in denial.

THE *IN-LOVE* DRUG

Romance is truly one of the most exotic spices of life. Without it, life is as bland as a potato without butter and salt. You can subsist on a plain potato but you won't really experience the pleasure life offers. Western cultures are obsessed with the butter and salt of romance. (We cluck our tongues in distain at the thought of arranged marriage.) So ingrained is the spiced-up notion of romance, we ignore the fact that it is a human artifice, its definition as unromantic as that bland potato. Alas, romance is a social construct, a label invented by humans to describe a certain group of powerful emotions and specific behaviors associated with human mating rituals.

The *In- love* stage (see the box below) is the most piquant, the most compelling of all emotions associated with romance. **As an emotion (like all thought, for that matter) it is caused by a chemical reaction[©] that takes place in the**

brain. Of course, we've all heard about the infamous *chemistry* between two people. This well-known kind of chemistry has always referred to only one aspect of love: physical attraction. And while physical attraction is plenty powerful in itself, the kind of chemical reactions I'm talking about it much broader, more complex, and more compelling than just physical attraction.

Important: The *In-Love* part is the infatuation stage, the giddy stage where you can't get enough of the person. The loving part is the *attachment stage*; the part where you're bonded to someone so that they are an integral part of you but the intense high is gone. Attachment has it's own set of chemicals. (More about attachment later.)

Nature designed this two-stage process as a means of species survival. Nature dumps the *In-Love* chemicals (*I-L Drugs*) into our blood stream so that we will mate in order to procreate. The attachment chemicals are designed to keep us mated long enough to raise our young.

Brain research in the last two decades has identified the specific neurotransmitters (brain chemicals) responsible for what we call love. It turns out that **the brain in love is quite**

♥ Want details? See *Molecules of Emotion* by Candace Pert.

like the brain on cocaine. What we call love, in the most unromantic of notions, is caused by neurotransmitters (hormones are one kind of neurotransmitter) circulating around in the brain, creating a mental and physical craving. Ever been so totally preoccupied by thoughts of another person that you can barely function? Can barely wait to be with the person? Feel physically sick if you're not around that person? Then, when you're finally with them, you feel giddy, energized, joyous, optimistic and well...high as a kite. (Any similarity to drug addicted behavior is purely intentional).

When people are on drugs like cocaine, alcohol, or marijuana, their judgment is impaired...so impaired that often they don't have the mental capacity to know they're impaired. So it is with being in love. The saying *Love is Blind* is still as true to today as when Shakespeare wrote it, (although technically he was really referring to being *In-Love.*) It doesn't matter how educated or how much experience you've had, once you've inhaled the love drug, you're vulnerable to its compulsion.

LOVE'S LUNACY

The folly of human behavior during the *In-Love* phase has remained the subject of most all poetry, literature, song, movies, TV, and now blogs throughout recorded history. This subject is so gripping because it epitomizes a universal experience: We've all been there, done that. **We're drawn to stories about love's lunacy because they make us feel better about being the imperfect human we are**. Misery really does love company. The daily soap operas are a perfect example. Despite the derisive sneers they invoke, millions of people watch the daily melodramas. Those who sneer the most about the daytime dramas are usually tuned-in to the "more acceptable" nighttime melodramas. Note the popularity of *Desperate Housewives*. Advise columns are read for the same reason. And now it is reality shows with real people acting foolish in front of millions.

Look at the list below. Is this not the dramatic theme of advice columns, TV and movie scripts, poetry, and novels? And haven't you been in your own personal drama at some time in your life?

What has been your particular ⊠ ?
Here's a checklist
<u>You Fell In-Love With Someone:</u>
✓ Unavailable or didn't love you back
✓ In debt up to their eyeballs

- ✓ Who was a tightwad
- ✓ Abusive
- ✓ Who has never been able to be faithful
- ✓ With an existing family
- ✓ Too old or too young
- ✓ With huge emotional baggage
- ✓ Addicted to drugs, alcohol, gambling, or sex
- ✓ Irresponsible with money
- ✓ Unable to keep a job
- ✓ With extreme fluctuations of mood
- ✓ Overly self-centered
- ✓ With low self-esteem (overly dependent and sensitive to criticism)
- ✓ Socially inept
- ✓ Who is a control freak
- ✓ Who talks too much or not at all
- ✓ Who can't tolerate being alone
- ✓ Obsessive
- ✓ Overly possessive
- ✓ Chronically negative
- ✓ With no common interests
- ✓ With opposing religious, cultural, or political background
- ✓ With very different moral values
- ✓ Who literally came back from the dead[A]

[⊗] It happens in the soaps!

I could go on and on and still not hit your particular situation, but you get the point. As a relationship counselor for twenty plus years, I heard couple after couple (no longer high on love) lament on and on about one or more of these behaviors in their spouse. As an unemotional observer, I was able to see the common denominator in all these couples:

- ✓ They didn't see it coming at all or
- ✓ They denied or excused away the magnitude of the problem in the beginning and, <u>most importantly</u>…
- ✓ They resisted taking responsibility for their choice, blaming the partner for the unacceptable behavior.

In all cases, they were blind-sided by the drug-induced high of the *In-Love* stage and made life-changing decisions based on impaired judgment. Once the *In-Love* drug had subsided, they were faced with: OOPS! **What You See is What You Get!**

It's very characteristic of human behavior to feel victimized when blind-sided. So, even though these individuals had voluntarily entered into the relationship, they universally felt like they had been duped. What naturally comes next is a combination of one or more of the following: bewilderment, anger, resentment, depression, frustration and BLAMING…any of which smothers the few lingering *In-Love* chemicals.

Family and friends close to the *In-Love* couple often see what the couple can't. Outsiders are not blind but ARE in a bind. Verbalizing reservations risks losing a bond. And most often it's futile anyway. People *In-Love* develop a **listening deficiency**.

A CASE OF LISTENING DEFICIENCY

Janet and Randy are my most memorable couple because it all played out in front of me. In most counseling situations, I come in after the fact. Not in this case.

Janet was an attractive 45 years old very successful accountant. She had been divorced for 10 years. She had no children. She hated being single and was beyond frustration at not being able to find a "good" man. Usually extremely confident and competent, Janet's frustration in the romance department had led to bouts of self-blame, the usual consequence of which is depression.

Randy was a 46 year-old businessman whose business was currently in trouble. Although quite physically attractive and socially outgoing, Randy lacked intrinsic self-esteem. Randy was a closet namby-pandy. As soon as there was a hint his business was heading in a southern direction, his wife decided going south was a very good idea. She got the good lawyer while Randy procrastinated. Not surprisingly, she got the house as well as a chunk of alimony before there was none to get, leaving Randy

---

with an income that afforded him a rented studio apartment.

Janet was my 2 p.m. client. Randy was my 3 p.m. client. You see it coming, right? It was Janet that initiated the idea. She wanted to know who the good-looking man in the waiting room was...she thought she had seen him somewhere before. I told her it was confidential information. I sensed what she was up to so I also said, TRUST ME, THIS IS NOT A GOOD IDEA, JANET!!!

Janet, being the determined person that she was, cast my advice to the wind. Instead, she racked her brain until she thought she remembered where she'd seen him before. She suddenly decided that being at the Chamber of Commerce breakfast meetings would be great for business. Four weeks after I warned her away from Randy, she had managed (against even stronger warnings) to get a date with him. Another two weeks and she was smitten. "I found a good, kind man," Janet protested. "Why are you so opposed to us as a couple?"

What's a therapist to do? Janet was In-Love and I knew she would ignore the reasons even if I could give them to her, which I couldn't, because my work with Randy was confidential. Janet's depression not-so-mysteriously vanished. Meantime, namby-pandy Randy was happily going along for the ride, also against advice.

I urged Janet to give it more time. What I got was the boot. Within 6 weeks after they had their first date, the gaga twosome could no longer see a reason to spend good money on a therapist who wasn't in their corner. Within 6 months the invitation arrived (a need to show how wrong I was???). It took only 20 months of marriage before the high-flying couple took a nosedive.

To her credit, Janet swallowed her pride and showed up in my office. They were living in Janet's home and Randy's business was on the chopping block. "He can't make a decision, he doesn't carry his weight, he's more in debt than I realized," she lamented. "He won't communicate with me. He sulks when he doesn't get his way instead of standing up for himself. He wouldn't even come here with me. It's worse than with my first husband." With a possibility of another divorce in her future, Janet was more depressed than ever.

Being right is sometimes a case of sad not glad.

THE MUST OF LUST

Who hasn't committed a major ⊠ caper in the throws of the most powerful drug of all: lust? The *In-Lust* chemicals are different than the *In-Love* chemicals but often act in conjunction with their love counterparts....but not always! Just about anyone can think of someone who confused the two, usually with great regret down the road. They have unfamiliar and very unsexy sounding names.© Despite the unsexy names, **there is absolutely nothing more contributory to impaired judgment and listening deficiency than sexual mesmerism.**

Lust is the sense of urgency that comes from a combination of sex drive and sexual arousal;

♥ nitric acid, serotonin, dopamine, epinephrine, norepinephrine, oxytocin, cortisol, pheromone, and prolactin.

the difference between the two is explained below. The *In-Lust* drugs are the most powerful during the procreating years, less so in mid life, and continue their downward trend with aging. However, they have been known to make a cameo appearance even in the last decades of life... if under the spell of being *In-Lust*. Never underestimate the power of lust no matter what you age!!!

I once counseled an 85 year-old widower whose wife had been dead for fifteen years. He told me his sex drive had died with his wife. Sans sex for all these years, he came to see me for advice because he was now madly in-love and equally in-lust with a 65 year-old woman. Even thought the sex part really scared him after all the years of celibacy, the lust drive was compelling enough for him to see a counselor.

Advertisers certainly know the power of lust. So do novelists, screenwriters, songwriters and even religious leaders... just about anyone who wants to get us to buy something or to influence us in some way. Here's the front-page news, though: <u>Lust could care less whether it's glorified or condemned; it's exhilarating high remains undeniable.</u> The primitive, commanding nature of lust laughs in the face of promised monogamy, unwanted conception, religious doctrines, age or cultural differences, or any other social obstacles. Lust easily jumps any man-made hurdle put in its way. In the game of species survival, lust will win, hands down. **Biology doesn't care whether you're compatible or happy over the long haul.** Even if procreation is out of the question, when the lust chemicals are circulating in your blood stream, you're a patsy for the gremlins that can make you lose all sensibility.

EXTRA! EXTRA! READ ALL ABOUT IT!
Social power linked to lust
ANYCITY, USA-- In a truly shocking discovery of events, President Foolish, Governor Righteous, and Reverend Hypocrite were caught red-handed using the services of

prostitutes. The big buzz on the street:

Behind the Wheel of Sex Drive
Here are some <u>general</u> truths about heterosexual sex drive:

➢ Sexual drive is thought of as the frequency of interest in sexual activity

➢ Testosterone is the major hormone (neurotransmitter) responsible for sex drive in both males and females.

- Male sex drive is stronger than the female's.
- Male sex drive ebbs more slowly with age.
- Female sex drive is more complicated, apparently being intertwined with feeling "connected".
- Menopause can wreck havoc on sex drive, but not always.
- Sex drive and sexual arousal are two distinct entities and can act independently of each other. (more about sexual arousal later).

Important: Current thinking is that sex drive is genetically programmed; the amount and kinds of neurotransmitters responsible for sex drive is predetermined. Like many genetic traits this means an individual has a <u>predisposition</u> for a certain sex drive level. A predisposition can be enhanced or inhibited by experience…both nature and nurture determines the final drive level.

Sex drive can be infuriating.

It can smack you in the groin when you least expect it, when you don't want it, when it will certainly get you in trouble. Conversely, when you most need it, it can mysteriously vanish.

Not tonight, dear.

During the *In-Love-In-Lust* phase of a relationship, sex drive can seem very partner compatible, only to discover months or years down the road it has become a battleground of differences.

For some individuals sex drive is illusory, never bowling them over. Individuals with low sex drive are puzzled about all the hype. Low-sexed individuals usually hide in the shadows for fear of ridicule from a society obsessed with all things sexual.

Then there are the hyper-sexed individuals who can't seem to get enough; they can also be shadow seekers. We have a lovely names for them: sex addicts, nymphomaniacs, or satyrists.

Society has an ill-defined level of sexual drive acceptability, but too low or too high and you're a weirdo.

Rousing Sexual Arousal

Sexual arousal has its own unique combination of chemicals that act on the sympathetic and parasympathetic nervous systems to cause physical changes in the body. As with sex drive it has a genetic component and its final profile as an adult is vulnerable to life experience in the early years of human development.

Here are some <u>general</u> truths about heterosexual sexual arousal:

- ➤ It is an emotional and physiological response to individualistic sexual stimuli.
- ➤ It is possible for the two to act independently of each other; i.e., an individual can be emotionally aroused but alas, not have the desired physical response. (Enter Viagra & others!)
- ➤ Sexual stimuli that cause arousal are as varied as the imagination and once established become hard-wired, i.e., if paper dolls turn you on, they will remain arousing throughout the sexual lifespan.
- ➤ Anxiety can enhance or hinder sexual arousal.
- ➤ Male arousal has a strong visual component.
- ➤ Male arousal is anthropologically linked to reproductive capacity; an hourglass

figure is a signal of this capacity and is most arousing for most men.

➤ Female arousal has a strong verbal component.

➤ Female arousal is anthropologically linked to security; a male who is a good provider is most arousing for most women.

➤ As with sex drive, female arousal is more complicated and more vulnerable to an emotional component.

Anxiety and Sexual Arousal

Western society has sacked sex with more expectations and taboos than a porcupine has quills, making ballooning sexual arousal thin-skinned and easy deflated by the prick of the slightest no-no. Shrouded in clouds of rights and wrongs, arousal is often fogged by anxiety.

Because sexual arousal is a chemical response, it is particularly vulnerable to anxiety's chemical base: adrenaline. Adrenaline in the blood stream before and/or during sexual arousal can act like a wet blanket on a fire, but it can

How can so much pleasure cause so much angst?

also act like oxygen on that fire. Example: Some individuals find sexual recklessness exciting, others are turned-off by the exact same reckless event.

A SOAP BOX DISCOURSE ON SEXUAL DEVELOPMENT

The exasperating nature of sex drive and sexual arousal has much to do with its genetic basis and the ensuing years of development. As I mentioned, an individual's particular DNA determines a predisposition at birth but it is NOT fully formed yet. <u>The next 8 years of life are considered critical periods and are crucial to brain development.</u>[©] It is during these 8 years that the main nerve connections that determine sexuality are being mapped; it is also during these years that the map is most vulnerable to adrenaline.

Think of a brain as a map of the United States.[a] At birth the neural connections are like the main interstate highways connecting the major cities to each other. The experiences

---

♥ See *Lovemaps* by John W. Money, Ph.D.
♠ See *The Three- Pound Enigma* by Sharon Moffett, Ph.D.

we have after birth add more and more side roads, all connecting one to another. Most of the side roads are added in the first third of life but new roads can be developed at any age... as long as new experiences are inputted. The ability of the brain to add new neurons is called brain plasticity.

Sadly, most societies rejects any thought that a child might be a <u>continuingly</u> developing *sexual* human being. We barely allow ourselves to accept that adolescence triggers a sexual component. This is a tragedy because it ignores the vulnerability of sexual development in the early years. The **final** brain chemicals and the neurons that transport them shape who we are as an adult sexual being and are mainly determined by the experiences we have in those first eight years.

Admonishing or even worse, punishing, a child for sexual curiosity has the potential for scarring him or her for life. It's a sad fact, though, that simple neglect of sexual development is the culprit most often responsible for adult sexual woes.

Here an example of how we neglect childhood sexual development. Children learn social behaviors by watching their parents and others as well as by verbal instruction. If you want a child to be polite, then you have to act polite in the family home and verbally encourage the child...as in "say thank you, Johnny." When it comes to sex, however, we hide most all examples. It is okay to have a peck on the cheek, but deep kissing in front of children is considered a taboo. That parents have sexual intercourse is probably the best-kept secret of all. Children don't need to *see* parents have sexual intercourse but they do need to *learn* that it is a normal and acceptable event between them.

Open, natural conversations about sexuality are considered okay only when a child is "old enough" to understand. This is often way too late. The playground of life (and now the internet) is usually way ahead of parents.

ATTACHMENT'S CONNECTION

➜   **BA Humbug!**

Here is the news that no one wants to hear: the high of *In-Love/In-Lust* chemicals doesn't last.   No matter how many candles you light or how many date nights you have, you cannot keep the I-L chemical in peak performance much past 18 months.

Well, if that true...then what???????

Rest assured. Nature has not deserted us. When the *In-Love/In-Lust* drugs begin to dissipate, a new set of drugs take their place.

These are the drugs of attachment. Captained by oxytocin, these chemicals navigate the ship of mating through the inevitable rough waters of long-term relationships. While oxytocin is really the attachment drug, it is more commonly thought of as the *Love* drug. It is the drug that allows you to deeply love someone at the same time you can be furious, exasperated, even disgusted with them. Oxytocin and its relatives act as the glue that binds…and a strong glue it is too! It doesn't abandon us as easily as the *In-Love/In-Lust* drugs. It can and often does remain with us throughout a lifetime, despite difficult and trying times.

Important. Oxytocin is also the drug that is responsible for the love (attachment) we feel for our children, friends, family. Appreciate, please, the sophisticated nature of this drug. We love our mates, our children, our family, and our friends, but we love each of them in different and refined ways.

Not Invincible

As strong as it is, Oxytocin is not unassailable. It can be slowly eroded by long-term disappoint, resentment, guilt, betrayal and other negative emotions. And to the heartbreak of millions, oxytocin can also be eclipsed by a surge of the *In-Love/In-Lust* drugs for a new person. *Note: eclipsed is not the same as replaced or eroded.* **It is possible to be attached to one person while still In-Love/In-Lust with another because different but co-existing chemicals cause the two emotions.**

Perhaps because this apparent enigma is so tormenting for all involved and so universally experienced, there is no other reality as chronicled by writers.

However, when you strip this *apparent enigma* down to its chemical origins, it is really not such a mystery. Novelty is a potent chemical force in the make-up of humans. New and exciting experiences generate many of the very same chemicals that are present during the *In-Love/In-Lust* phase. The chemical thrill of novelty is why we have evolved from the single cell animal to the multi-celled, complex, forward thinking human being we are today. Not surprisingly, we're bewitched by the chemical flow that occurs when we encounter new and shiny anything, from cars to food to better mousetraps, to different partners.

Which brings to mind the intriguing question: does© nature really design human beings to be

---

♥ I'm using the present tense because nature is continually evolving, not static.

monogamous for life? This is a question that promotes passionate debate on both sides. Rather than debate this, perhaps the better question might be: does nature design all human beings the same? This question is not debatable. Each life may be equal in value but this certainly does not mean people are the same. It does mean some individuals are genetically programmed to do better with monogamy than others.

1+1=2 = Forever ?

If monogamy is important to you, consider the following:

- Visionary people have brains that are programmed to crave the novelty chemicals more than less creative people.
- The brain chemicals of power, like those of novelty, are similar to the *I-L* chemicals. Remember the banner headline earlier on: Social Power Linked to Lust?
- The chemical of danger and risk are also similar to the *I-L* chemicals; some humans are pre-programmed to crave danger and risk.

Does this mean that creative and/or powerful and/or risk-taking people are unlikely to remain faithful to one partner? No research that I know of proves it, but I would treat it as a red flag. It is certainly something to think about, especially if the person has a history of serial monogamous relationships. And especially if the person is a triple threat:

Creative, Powerful, and a major Risk-Taker. Triple threat people are less likely to be influenced by social norms, sometimes even believing the norms don't apply to them.

Don't think you're safe, however, if the potential partner you have in mind (or your current partner) is none of the above. Everyone is vulnerable to the drugs of novelty and anyone can succumb to the spell of the *I-L* Drugs. Not to worry... the majority of people are susceptible to guilt, fear, humiliation, uncertainty, loyalty, integrity, self-image, children, money, and oxytocin, some of the potent antidotes to the *I-L* Drugs.

For sure, the movie stars, musicians, athletes, politicians, and religious leaders get a lot of press when they break their vows of monogamy. Are we so interested in the escapades of famous people because we're comforted by knowing they are, in the end, more like us than not?

SLIM PICKINGS

There is still one aspect left of love and lust that does remain a mystery: why we are attracted to a *particular* person. Other than pheromone, researches have not discovered brain chemicals that are responsible for particular mate selection. Pheromone is an odorless chemical well known in the animal kingdom for contributing to mate selection. It is usually secreted during the mating cycle.

And while the perfume industry would like you to believe they have the ability to capture the essence of *human* pheromone, respected scientists remain skeptical.

Just about everyone has a first hand experience with the exasperating reality of being surrounded by many potential mates but coming up empty handed. Everywhere people are looking to make a connection: school, work, organizations, clubs, bars, single dating events, and computer dating sites. Possibilities abound, yet nothing clicks. One of my female clients was so frustrated by this reality that she decided to try an experiment. She was a health nut so she placed herself on the sideline about midway through the route of a giant 10K race. She figured that there was no better place to find a large sample of fit men. Hundreds of men passed by her. Still, she claimed not one of them sparked an interest.

You might wish to pass her off shallow because she was going solely on physical attributes. To say she was shallow to select a mate mainly on physical attributes is to say the human race is shallow. Like it or not, this is the way the vast majority of humans determine a "person of interest." The most curious result of her experiment is the sheer number of men that didn't pass muster. How is that possible? It's too simple to say she is just too picky. **Our reasons for being attracted to a particular person are complicated by the fact that they are mostly unconscious. Infuriating but true.**

Here are some general known factors in mate selection:

❖   Choice is highly idiosyncratic; you might find a person attractive while your friend is yawning with total disinterest.

❖   There is some characteristic(s) about the person that allows you to idealize them.

❖   The idealize notion fits into a subconscious fantasy about what that person can provide you. Just a few examples are: security, romance, social status, excitement, power, sexual ecstasy, intellectual stimulation, devotion, domination, discipline, submission, and insecurity.

❖   You project this fantasy onto another person, mainly as a result of their physical attributes. Regardless of the many warning, we **do judge a book by its cover.**

❖   Your unique fantasy is a product of your genetic make-up combined with your early childhood experiences.

Important. A reminder. In childhood, neural connections are being formed that later create fairly rigid patterns. These patterns are unconscious to us. So, while we may consciously think we want one kind of partner, our brains have been trained to be comfortable with what is familiar. For example, if you came from a highly disciplined home that drove you crazy, your conscious brain may tell you to select a partner that is a free spirit, only to discover months down the road that their lack of orderliness drives you crazy.

A MATCHED PAIR?

In February of 2008, PBS television presented a program called *Secrets of the Sexes* that detailed a scientific experiment in which a zoologist, an experimental psychologist, and an evolutionary biologist tried to predict mates for 50 men and 50 women looking for love. The zoologist used facial similarities to predict matches. The psychologist used a CQ (compatibility quotient) to predict his matches while the biologist used a physical attraction rating from the participants. The experiment used a speed-dating format where each gender first met with all 50 of the opposite gender participants for 30 seconds. During that time they didn't speak but rated the person's physical attractiveness. Next, they repeated the process spending 3 minutes getting to know each other. Finally, each participant selected his or her choices for a desired date, hoping that their choices would also pick them. All of the participants found a least one mutual match, most 2 or 3 matches, and one woman found 10 matches.

Not surprisingly, the experiment determined that the 3 minutes of conversation had little to do with the participant's choice of matches. All the participants selected their choices within moments of sitting across from the other person based solely on physical attributes.

The matched couples then had the opportunity to go on dates to see if they liked each.

The results? Not a single success. Not one couple wanted a second date. The three scientists admitted failure with their predictions, but did offer this conclusion: successful matching is based on something primitive, something originating deep within the psyche and formulated early in childhood.

represent the whole person©. Go ahead and pick up the book because of its cover…just don't stop there. There is no better way to keep from making a heart-breaking mistake then by reading the entire book. Keep in mind, though, that the only way to really know someone's true character is to read between the lines. There is a saying that holds true when it comes to really knowing a person: *Action speaks louder than words*. In other *words*, don't believe what a person says, believe only in what they do. If a person says they love you, care about you, desperately need you but is physically or verbally abusive, that person is not capable of healthy love no matter how many times the say it. If a person claims that you are more important to them then their pals, but consistently chooses to spend time with their friends, that person values their friends more than you. If a person promises they are going to stop smoking, over-eating, get more exercise but doesn't do any of these, their words are meaningless. If a person rarely says I love you, but is giving, thoughtful, respectful, loyal, and understanding, then you can count on their love. **Forget about what a person says or doesn't say… the only thing that really counts in life is what a person <u>does</u>**. Words are easy while actions are not.

♥ Sad to say but many enjoyable, rewarding chapters go "unread" because we weren't attracted to the cover.

Remember, in the *I-L* phase, people see what they want to see, what their fantasy projects onto the other person. It is almost impossible to read between the lines of a person during the *I-L* phase. It is only after the *I-L* Drugs have settled down that you have the ability to know what you're getting. **So, waiting at least a minimum of 18 months, preferably 2 years, before making any major changes in your life, is the best way to know a person's true character.**

Yes, this waiting period can be impractical. Yes, lust is compelling. Yes, biological clocks can be ticking. Yes, financial belts can be tightening. Yes, yes, yes, there are tons of "reasonable" reasons that people are quick to move in together or get married. Not one of these reasons will seem reasonable in retrospect, however, if you find yourself emotionally, legally, and financially mired down in a miserable life. The waiting period is no panacea, no guarantee that you will be one of the lucky few truly happy with their choice of mate for an entire lifetime. Waiting, however, is the one option you have that is free and accessible. Couple counseling is another option, usually one that is very expensive and totally dependent on the quality of the counselor that you get. Of course, you would have to LISTEN to your counselor.

Another way to read between the lines is to give due diligence to the person's biography. Have they been married multiple times? What was their childhood like? How do they get along with their family? How do you get along with their family? If they came from a chaotic, dysfunctional family, this is worth your consideration.

None of these are reasons for an automatic discard. There isn't a person alive who came from a perfect family and these days divorce is common. Still, paying attention to a person's history is a better way of predicting the future than depending on your subconscious fantasy. The difficult part is to pay attention to the warning signs and not find excuses to disregard them. Like it or not, **Love does not conquer all.**

In an ideal world, the best way to select a mate would be to know yourself…to surface your fantasy. Easier said then done. There are lots of self-help books on the market designed to assist you in your self-discovery journey and some people have success with the self-help trip. Psychotherapy is another way, either individual or group. As mentioned, this can be expensive and is dependent on the quality of the therapist.

Alas, most people muddle through on trail and error; an excellent, if often painful, learning method that works only if people heed the learning opportunities.

DUMPEE-FLU

The end of a relationship is never a pretty picture. Even if it is a mutual decision, it is always a highly emotional time. The picture gets really ugly, however, if the *I-L* drugs are still in the system when the relationship goes south. The brain *In-Love* is like the brain on cocaine, remember? Take away the cocaine and the brain goes through withdrawal symptoms. **The body's response to being stripped of the *I-L* drugs is akin to a miserable case of what is best described as Dumpee Flu (DF). If you fall victim to DF, the body and psyche feel like they are in a ever-tightening vise, a merciless experience rarely forgotten.**

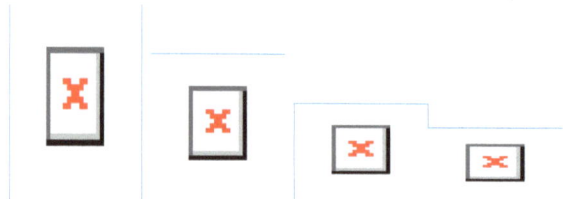

The physical pain is most often felt in the mid torso area and is experienced as either stomach and/or heart© pain. Nausea, vomiting, uncontrollable shaking, fever, low energy, deep sadness, lack of concentration, obsession, insomnia, loss of appetite, and bouts of crying are common symptoms and are sometimes accompanied by suicidal thoughts. Most people feel a need to isolate themselves, as being around non DF people tends to bring on sadness and feelings of disassociation from the real world.

Even after years of a relationship and all the *I-L* Drugs are long gone, withdrawal of the attachment drug of oxytocin and its relatives can bring on a bad case of DF. In general, the symptoms aren't as acute as the withdrawal of the *I-L* Drugs, but the malaise and despair can still be quite miserable.

Desperation to get rid of the symptoms can and often does make people do mindless, shortsighted, and later regretful acts. From begging, to stalking, to calling and hanging up, to burning up reminders, to grilling mutual friends, to thoughts or even acts of revenge, the list is long and sordid.

♥ Perhaps the reason we so associate love with the heart rather than the brain.

CUPID'S POISON

Going in, cupid's arrow feels good. Alas, coming it out it leaves a deep, painful wound. For the vast majority of people, time heals the wound. Unfortunately, some wounds are deep enough to heal only on the surface, while underneath the wounds festers. In some severe cases, it is not an exaggeration to say that the intensity of the emotions felt can create a case of post-traumatic-stress. Post-traumatic-stress (PTS) is a result of the brain being "scarred" by the intensity of emotions. Intense negative emotions create deep pathways in the brain, which make it likely that similar events in the future will cause neurons to travel down the same pathways. That's why, say a loud backfire of a car on a city street, can cause a war-warped veteran to react as if he is in the midst of a gun battle.

A person who had suffered through a really bad case of DF may find future relationship or even contemplation of future relationships extremely stressful. After a really miserable case of DF, a person may avoid any commitment for years. Some people may never be able to fully commit to another person due to an unconscious fear of losing that person and going through DF.

The more unanticipated the ending of a relationship, the worse the case of DF is likely to be. Pretending that the relationship is hunky-dory and then suddenly ending it, is not a way to "protect" the feelings of another person. It is a bogus excuse to avoid confrontation and will only cause a worse case of DF for the surprised victim. And while years of fighting in a relationship can be a sad way to live, in a perverse way the anger and resentment makes it easier to separate in the end. People who no longer like each other have much milder case of DF; some avoid it all together and feel nothing but a great sense of relief.

Important: While it can be miserable to be the dumpee, it is not a cakewalk for the dumper. People who have been together for any length of time have attachments. And while it would be foolish to feel sorry for the dumper, it would be equally foolish to hold fast to the belief that the dumper might not feel sad, regretful, disloyal, and guilt ridden.

TIME HEALS ALL WOUNDS

The all-consuming phase of DF usually lasts 2 to 6 weeks. Slowly, it does get better. The intense physical symptoms lessen with each passing day. Feelings of sadness, anger, confusion, obsession, and disassociation diminish with time as the brain chemicals dissipate©. Most people are feeling more normal within 6 months. For sure, 6 months is a big chunk of time out of a person's life, but is an inescapable fact of life that nature does not give up easily.

Remember, the symptoms of DF are so miserable that most people become obsessed with getting the person back into their life just to keep from hurting. **However, any contact with the person who gave you DF will bring you back to zero in the healing process.** This includes visual sightings, phone calls and emails. Please heed: begging only makes you look pathetic, not a pretty picture. If the dumper gives in to your begging, it will be out of guilt. Do you really want to be with someone who stays with you not because of love but because of guilt?

On it's way out, Cupid's arrow plays dirty tricks on you. *It turns out that the best medicine is your own resolve*. Ironically, when you most need resolve, you are knocked

---

♥ In actuality, it's the returning to normal of the *I-L* receptor sites in the brain.

to your knees by the "poison" left by the arrow.

It's not much consolation for a person with the awful symptoms of DF to know it is going to get better. In the throws of an acute episode, you don't feel better hearing that down the road the person who gave you DF will only be a blip on the radar screen of your life. Yet, keeping these truths in forefront of your mind, is where you get the necessary resolve.

ANTIVENIN

Here comes the part where you get the list of Do's and Don'ts designed to counteract the venom. On the surface, a list, which is just a bunch of words, makes anything look easy. The words, however, command action or in some cases non-action. The difficult part is getting your brain to act on the list when you're *under the influence* of the arrow's poison. Being dumped feels like you've been bitten by a rattlesnake and you're alone in the desert. You have to crawl miles in the hot desert sun to get to an emergency room where you can get the life-saving antivenin. You're alone, scared, weakened and physically sick. Can you do it?

Here's your challenge:
DON'T (NO! NO! NO!)

- Have <u>any</u> kind of contact with the dumper.
- Resort to mind-numbing drugs, legal or illegal. You have to feel the pain to get over it.
- Make yourself out to be the victim. Even if you did nothing worthy of being dumped, falling prey to the victim role will lengthen your mourning period and make you into a bitter, unsympathetic person. Bad things happen to good people for no justifiable reason. Accept that and you'll be able to move on with your life.
- Give in to humiliation and close yourself off to friends and family.
- Pretend to yourself or others that you're not hurting. Not dealing with the pain is the most frequent cause of PTS. Strong emotions not dealt with don't just vanish; the chemicals that cause them remain dormant waiting to torment you at a later date.
- Take any revenge actions. You'll need your dignity later on when this person is a distant memory and you're asking yourself, "What was I thinking?"
- Watch romantic movies in which love conquers all. You know first hand it doesn't.

DO (YES! YES! YES!)

o Get angry, feel sad, feel afraid of being alone. These are legitimate emotions, different from feeling the poor, helpless wretch of a victim. Anger, sadness, and fear will dissipate while victimization has a way of lingering for a lifetime.

o Cry as often as possible. Get in the bathtub or shower and cry until you can't cry anymore. Cry again 5 minutes later if you need to. If you want to cry but can't, listen to "your" song, pull out a favorite picture, remember a vacation.

o Obsess as much as possible. Talk aloud about it to any person you can get to listen. If there is no one you can talk to or you've worn your friends out, write it down. Write: *I hate you* (or something much, much worse) a hundred, two hundred, or more times. This is especially effective during the middle of the night when you can't sleep. Stay away from writing thoughts like, "How could you do this to me?" You'll slip into the victim role.

o Remind yourself frequently that requited love is the only worthwhile love. Ask yourself again and again, "Would I really rather to be with someone who didn't love me than be alone?"

o Fantasy you're revenge. Write it out in vivid detail.

o Write the dumpee a nasty letter. Save yourself a stamp and your self-esteem; **do not** mail it.

- Put an image of the dumper on the wall. Throw darts at it. Impale a melon on a stick. Write the dumper's name on it. Take a baseball bat to it. Stabbing balloons with the dumper's name on it works too.
- Watch comedy movies that poke fun at dumpees. You'll see yourself in a different "light."
- Stay healthy. Sip on healthy shakes during the day if your appetite is gone. If you're not sleeping, take naps, easier to do after a good cry.
- Breathe!!! Air is free and always available. Deep breathing infuses your brain with oxygen and helps to reduce the stress chemicals. Take 20 deep breaths. Count them. Start over again if your mind wanders. This is particularly effective during sleepless nights or at any time you anticipate a panic or anxiety attack. Deep breathing is something you can do at work if you're having trouble with concentration. Trust me, the concentration needed to take 20 deep breaths is more difficult than it sounds …but it does work!
- Exercise. Research has shown that a 10 minute brisk walk can prevent an anxiety attack and drastically change a mood.

A FINAL NOTE

In the short-term, a romantic relationship is both magnetic and magical. In the long-term, romance evolves into a partnership that is both connection and cooperation. The evolution from bewitching to pragmatic is most often seamless, without a line of demarcation. You just wake up one day and it seems the magic is gone. What remains once the romance has been stripped of its veneer is your selection of a life partner; THE someone to share the inevitable roller coaster ride that we know as life. Do your due diligence on selecting that partner and the ride will be bumpy but gratifying beyond anything else life has to offer.